I0812437

A SHORT BIOGRAPHY OF WASHINGTON IRVING

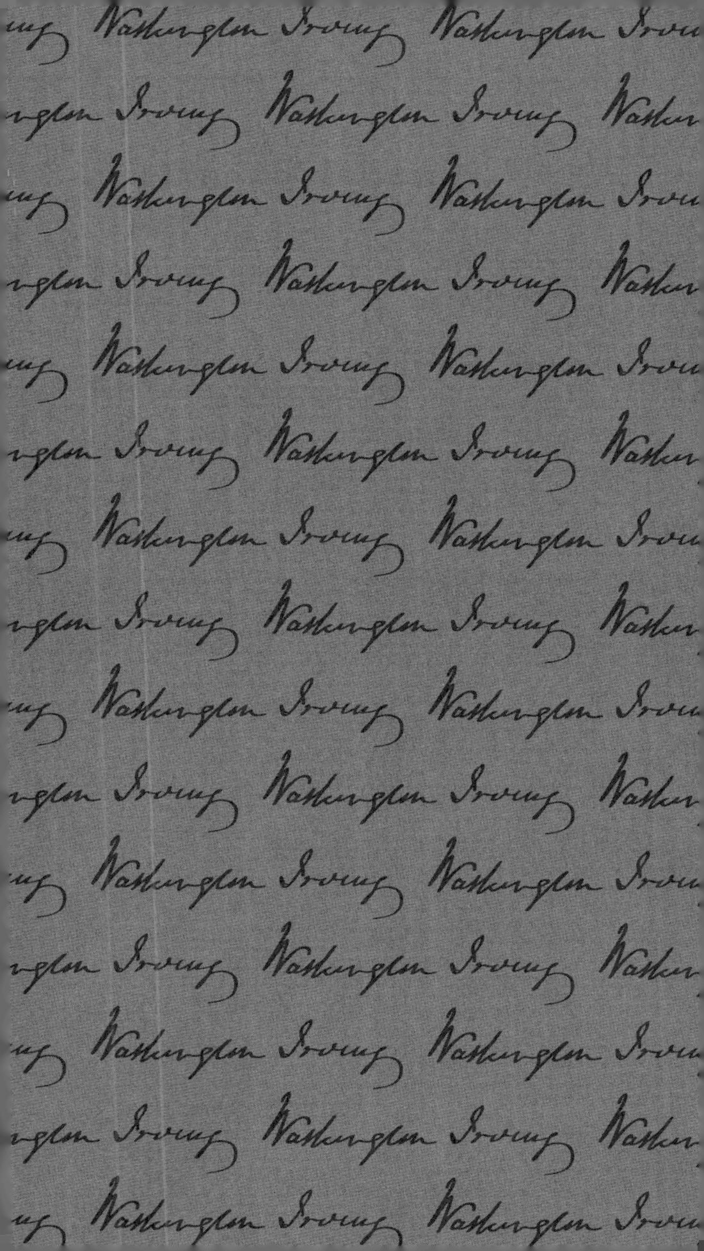
Washington Irving

A SHORT BIOGRAPHY OF Washington Irving

Henri-Pierre Corbacho

BENNA BOOKS
A Boutique Press for Artists & Writers
Carlisle, Massachusetts

A Short Biography of Washington Irving

Series Editor: Susan DeLand
Written by: Henri-Pierre Corbacho

For Richard, my rock
For Jeanne-Marie, my roots

978-1-944038-22-9

Front cover: John Wesley Jarvis (American, 1780–1840)
Washington Irving (American 1783–1859)
New York, 1809
Oil on panel
Historic Hudson Valley, Pocantico Hills, NY (SS.62.2 a-b)
Back cover: *Washington Irving and His Literary Friends at Sunnyside,* 1864,
Christian Schussele and Felix Darley, oil on canvas
National Portrait Gallery, Smithsonian Institution
Left to right: Henry T. Tuckerman, William Gilmore Simms, Oliver Wendell Holmes, Fitz Greene Halleck, Nathaniel Hawthorne, Henry Wadsworth Longfellow, Nathaniel Parker Willis, William H. Prescott, Washington Irving, James K. Paulding, Ralph Waldo Emerson, William Cullen Bryant, John P. Kennedy, J. Fenimore Cooper, and George Bancroft

Published by Benna Books
an imprint of Applewood Books, Inc.
Carlisle, Massachusetts

To request a free copy of our current catalog
featuring our best-selling books, write to:
Applewood Books
P.O. Box 27
Carlisle, Massachusetts 01741
Or visit us on the web at: www.awb.com

10 9 8 7 6 5 4 3 2 1
MANUFACTURED IN THE UNITED STATES OF AMERICA

WASHINGTON IRVING WAS AN EARLY American writer, satirist, and cultural influencer. He was born on April 3, 1783, in New York City, near present-day Wall Street, the youngest son of Scottish and English immigrants. William Irving Sr. was a merchant from Orkney, a Scottish isle, and a petty officer in the British navy. Sarah Sanders was the daughter of an English clergyman from Cornwall. They married in 1761 and had eleven children, though only eight lived to adulthood. Washington was the youngest of the brood. William and Sarah and their young family had moved to the British colony of New York and settled in Manhattan, and they quickly became affiliated with the city's fast-growing business class. The Irvings supported the rebel cause during the American Revolution. The suspension of hostilities between the British and American armies ended with a treaty that declared this small portion of the New World an independent nation in the year of Washington Irving's birth. General George Washington, commander of the Continental army and soon to be president of the Constitutional Convention, was an American hero, and baby Irving was his namesake.

Irving's mother said: "Washington's work is ended and the child shall be named after him."

An important encounter in Washington Irving's life occurred in 1789. Young Irving, who was six years old, met and was blessed by the first American president during George Washington's inauguration in New York. Many years later, this unexpected meeting was memorialized in a watercolor painting by George Bernard Butler Jr. that can be seen today in Irving's home, Sunnyside, on the Hudson River in New York State.

Reputed to be his father's favorite, Washington grew up in an atmosphere of indulgence. He was an uninspired student and escaped a college education, which his father had required of his older sons. From an early age, Irving was influenced by the literary tastes of his older brothers William and Peter. He loved adventure stories, and one of the early books in his scattered reading was *Don Quixote,* which inspired in him a lifelong interest in Spain and the Spanish people. By the age of fourteen, Irving was attracted by the theater and would not hesitate to slip out of school, or sneak out of family prayer meetings, to attend local performances. He was fascinated by the upper class of New York City.

The Irving brothers attended Columbia College.

Concerned over the sudden epidemic of yellow fever in New York, Irving's parents sent him to a healthier climate upriver in 1798. Irving visited his friend James Kirke Paulding in Tarrytown, New York, and traveled to surrounding small towns. In the village of Sleepy Hollow, Irving learned of ghost stories and Dutch customs that inspired him and would influence his writing.

As a young man, he journeyed through the Hudson Valley, a region that piqued his imagination, and he spent time in the Catskill Mountains, later the setting for *Rip Van Winkle.*

After graduating from private school, Irving worked in a law office as an attempt to avoid the family merchant business, which he disliked. Irving was quickly bored by the law, and in 1802 he began writing reviews for the *New York Morning Chronicle* and the *Corrector,* two newspapers edited by his brother Peter. Using the pseudonym Jonathan Oldstyle, Irving submitted notes and critiques of New York's social and recreational events. This pseudonym was the first of many Irving would use during his literary life.

Irving maintained a close relationship with his family his entire life. Although little is known of his relationship with his father, he had great affection for his mother, sisters, and brothers, who had a great influence on young Irving. William, the eldest; Ebenezer; Peter; and John Treat helped and advised him throughout his life. He made several trips up the Hudson and another into Canada. In 1804, in poor health, Irving left for Europe, where he lived for two years. The trip was organized and paid for by his brothers. They believed that living abroad would be beneficial to Irving's fragile health and would also further his education.

His writing was well received and earned Irving praise.

Irving convalesced in a spa in Bordeaux, France, where he sought treatment for a lung ailment. He quickly recovered and traveled throughout Europe, swiftly mastering the art of informal conversation, a talent that would endear him to his hosts. Irving wrote: "I endeavor to take things as they come with cheerfulness," and, "When I cannot get a dinner to suit my taste, I endeavor to get a taste to suit my dinner." While traveling in Italy, Irving met American painter Washington Allston in Rome, and they quickly became friends.

Following this encounter with Allston, Irving was seduced, for a fleeting moment, by the idea of becoming a painter.

Irving returned to America and was readmitted to the bar, but again quickly lost interest. He fraternized with a group of young writers he called the "Lads of Kilkenny." In 1807, Irving and childhood friend James Paulding, one of the "lads," were in their early twenties, full of life, and very much inclined to mock New York high society. They published a literary magazine called *Salmagundi* composed of parodies, puns, invectives, and satires. Writing under the name of William Wizard and various other pseudonyms, Irving ridiculed New York's culture scene, as well as state and government affairs. In the seventeenth issue, Irving gave New York City the moniker Gotham, later memorialized in pop culture by the Batman comic series and films.

The magazine, printed only twenty times—whenever the authors had sufficient material to make up an issue—generated some success and increased Irving's mysterious reputation.

Aaron Burr, a founding father and Thomas Jefferson's vice president, was a contentious politician who killed Alexander Hamilton over barbed remarks during a failed run for governor of New York. He was also a renegade land-grabber. He put together an unauthorized military band to attempt to take Spanish land in Mexico. President Jefferson unsuccessfully brought him to trial for conspiring to invade a nation at peace with the United States. Irving wrote about Aaron Burr's trial in 1807 for the *Morning Chronicle,* his brother Peter's newspaper. His portrayal of Burr facing prosecution witness General James Wilkinson is riveting: Wilkinson "strutted into court…stood for a moment swelling like a turkey-cock. Burr turned his head, looked him full in the face with one of his piercing regards, swept his eye over his whole person from head to foot,

To Thomas Jefferson's fury, Burr was acquitted.

as if to scan his dimensions, then coolly resumed his former position."

In 1809, under the pseudonym Diedrich Knickerbocker, Irving wrote his first major book, *A History of New York from the Beginning of the World to the End of the Dutch Dynasty,* and became locally famous. It was a satirical comment on the Dutch occupation, a critique on the Jeffersonian democracy, and a mockery of literary history. Like *Salmagundi,* it was a mixture of humors written for a New York audience. Revising it in 1812, Irving inserted a dream sequence featuring St. Nicholas soaring over treetops in a flying wagon, a creation later named Santa Claus. Although *A History of New York* was highly successful, Irving did not write any more creative literature for the next six years.

Twenty-six-year-old Washington Irving was engaged to marry Matilda Hoffman, daughter of Josiah Ogden, a former New York attorney general who trained Washington in the law. Washington passed the bar in 1806, still a reluctant lawyer. Irving fell deeply in love with Matilda and described her as "lovely in person and mind, of the most gentle and engaging manners, and with a sensibility that mingled gracefully with a playful humor." Tragedy struck when Matilda contracted tuberculosis. For two months Washington stayed by her bedside, until her last breath was spent. Matilda Hoffmann died on April 26, 1809, at the age of eighteen. After her death Irving never became engaged again and never married. In response to an inquiry about why he had never married, Irving wrote: "For years I could not talk on the subject of this hopeless regret; I could not even mention her name, but her image was continually before me, and I dreamt of her incessantly."

Irving felt literature was a way to express himself, not a profession.

"There is a sacredness in tears. They are not the mark of weakness, but of power. They speak more eloquently

than ten thousand tongues. They are the messengers of overwhelming grief, of deep contrition, and of unspeakable love."

Irving was initially against the War of 1812, but when the nation's capital was attacked by the British, he decided to enlist in the armed services and became aide-de-camp to Daniel D. Tompkins, military governor of New York and later vice president to President James Monroe. During the next two years, Irving helped coordinate the New York war effort. The war was catastrophic for the Irving family business, and in 1815 Washington left for England to try to save P&E Irving and Company, the failing Liverpool branch of the family import-export business. His brother Peter had fallen ill, so Irving helped with the affairs of the firm, yet within three years, the company was bankrupt. Irving was now thirty-five and

Washington visited his sister, Sarah Van Wart, who lived in Birmingham, England.

without any means of support. He thought about earning his living by writing. Irving visited friends in Scotland, who encouraged him to continue to write. This gave Irving the confidence he needed to pursue his literary career.

While he was living in Birmingham, Irving wrote his most famous short story, *The Legend of Sleepy Hollow.* It tells the story of Ichabod Crane, the schoolmaster of the village, and his unfortunate attempt to win the heart and hand of Katrina Van Tassel; and of the Headless Horseman, a Revolutionary War soldier whose head was blown off by a cannonball. The ghost was often seen by the Old Dutch Church, where local historians say he was buried, and was believed to be eternally in search of his head. Irving composed another legendary story, *Rip Van Winkle,* overnight. In this Revolutionary War–era story, Rip Van Winkle is a Dutch American villager who, while in the Catskill Mountains,

***The Legend of Sleepy Hollow* is among the earliest examples of American fiction with enduring popularity.**

miraculously travels forward in time, sleeping through the War of Independence. Upon waking up, he discovers that he is decades into a future that is totally foreign to him. Irving created a folktale of the chapter in history when America went from colonies to a nation, with a story line that undoubtedly was more resonant than he realized. Published in New York in 1819, *The Legend of Sleepy Hollow* and *Rip Van Winkle* were contained in a collection of thirty-four essays and short stories entitled *The Sketch Book of Geoffrey Crayon, Gent.*, which was an immediate success. In fact, it was so well received that Irving decided to work on an edition for British readers.

The *Sketch Book* could perhaps be considered a traveler's guide to England, but it defines his desire to become a strong writer and recognized as such by the literary world.

Irving's reputation soared, and for the next two years he led an active social life in France, England, and Germany. Irving spent time in Dresden, Germany, where he sought medical advice for pains he suffered in his legs; befriended the wife of a diplomat; and updated *The Sketch Book* for a German publisher.

In 1825, Irving immersed himself in Spanish history and culture. For several months, he studied the language with a Spanish tutor. In 1826, while in Paris, Irving received an invitation from the American minister to Spain, Alexander Hill Everett, to visit him in Madrid. The minister had noted that several manuscripts related to the Spanish conquest of the Americas had just been released to the public, and he thought they might be of interest to Irving. After reading them, Irving started working on several books. *A History of the Life and Voyages of Christopher Columbus,* about the Italian explorer who sailed under the Spanish flag, took three years to write and was published in January 1828. As a follow-up, Irving then wrote *Voyages and Discoveries of the Companions of Columbus,* a meticulous account of the journeys taken by Columbus'

The Columbus book received rave reviews in the United States and Europe. Several editions were produced by the end of the nineteenth century.

travel companions and their exploration of the New World.

Granada is the Spanish word for pomegranate.

Irving traveled from Madrid to Granada, where he spent several months amassing materials on its history and conquest. He described the city as "a most picturesque and beautiful city, situated in one of the loveliest landscapes that I have ever seen." In 1829, Irving wrote *Chronicle of the Conquest of Granada*. The celebrated classic describes the struggle of Spanish sovereigns Ferdinand and Isabella against the Moors of the Kingdom of Granada, leading to the conquest in 1492. The story is based on historical documents and local archives.

In 1832, *Tales of the Alhambra* was published concurrently in the United States and England. Irving had requested access to the historic Alhambra Palace from the archbishop of Granada and the governor of the palace. Irving's notoriety and popularity facilitated his immediate access to the site, along with permission to live there. At that time, the Alhambra was not a national monument but a dirty, dilapidated edifice. The book magnificently combines legends, myths, and tales with real historical events, creating a brilliant story. While visiting Granada, Irving wrote observations and notes in his journals. Though not entirely certain his writing would convey the true beauty of the site and the awe it inspired in him, he wrote: "How unworthy is my scribbling of the place." The story contributed to reestablishing a connection between Western readers and the Alhambra. Interesting facts are worth noting: the city of Alhambra, California, is named after the book; and in 1950 a Spanish movie was based on the book. The publication of *Tales of the Alhambra* marked the end of Irving's journey through continental Europe.

In 1874, after reading the book, the daughter of Los Angeles developer Benjamin Wilson encouraged her father to use the name for the new city.

"Sweet is the memory of distant friends! Like the mellow rays of the

departing sun, it falls tenderly, yet sadly, on the heart."

In July 1829 Irving traveled to London, where he worked as aide-de-camp to American minister Louis McLane. Over the next year, Irving helped broker a trade agreement between the United States and the British West Indies. In 1830 Irving received a medal from the Royal Society of Literature and in 1831 was awarded an honorary doctorate of civil law from Oxford.

On May 21, 1832, after having achieved a strong literary reputation, Irving returned to New York, now a different city from the one he had left. Because of a steady headwind, Irving's return ship, the *Le Havre,* stalled outside New York Harbor. A local newspaper decided to dispatch a small sailboat to bring him ashore, a smart move that guaranteed the newspaper the exclusive coverage of Irving's return to America.

Irving recalls: "I passed through places that ought to be familiar to me, but all were changed."

Irving was soon reunited with family and friends, and the academic community and literary world welcomed him back with enthusiasm. Invitations for public dinners in his honor quickly followed.

Irving had been away from home for many years, and he reacquainted himself with America by traveling across the land. Within a year, he visited all but five of the twenty-four states in the Union. Irving then set out on a tour of some of the little-known territories off the western fringe of the country, taking him as far as Oklahoma. While visiting Missouri, Irving met with Chief Black Hawk and became critical of U.S. policy regarding the uprooting of Native American communities from their ancestral homelands. Irving wrote: "I find it extremely difficult, even when so near the seat of action, to get at the right story of these feuds between the White & Red Man, and my sympathies go strongly with the latter." In a letter to his brother Peter, Irving said that his visit to the western states had been "an opportunity of seeing the remnants of those great Indian tribes, which are now about to disappear as independent nations, or to be amalgamated under some new form of government." Soon after, Irving wrote *A Tour on the Prairies,* inspired by his travels on the frontier. The book was an immediate success in the United States. In 1834, American businessman, real estate investor, and founder of an American fur trade dynasty John Jacob Astor asked Irving to write about his Pacific Fur Company and its post on the Columbia River. In 1836, Irving finished writing *Astoria,* a fascinating account of Astor's land and sea adventures. When Astor died in 1848, Irving became executor of his estate. In his will, Astor had appointed Irving as first president of the Astor Library, later to be known as the New York Public Library. Irving kept this position until his death in 1859.

In 1811, a group of American traders built a fort at the mouth of the Columbia River, named Fort Astoria in honor of its financier, John Jacob Astor.

While visiting Astor, Irving met the French-born explorer and officer Benjamin Bonneville, whose orders were to collect information on the geography, geology, and topography of the country within the limits of the territories belonging to the United States. Bonneville showed Irving his maps of the land beyond the Rocky Mountains. Irving was fascinated by his tales of exploration.

Irving purchased Bonneville's maps and notes for $1,000.

James Fenimore Cooper, a popular American writer and Irving's contemporary, wrote historical fiction about frontier life and Native Americans in the western territories. Philip Freneau, called the "Poet of the American Revolution," joined Cooper in criticizing Irving for his extensive travels in England and Spain, saying he was now "more European than American." They both criticized Irving for his travels to England and Spain, asserting that he was now "more European than American." In 1837, in response to their

Irving did not appreciate his national loyalty being questioned.

criticism, he wrote a series of western books—*A Tour on the Prairies, Astoria,* and *The Adventures of Captain Bonneville.* Bonneville's journals and maps formed the backbone of the manuscript for the last of these.

Irving's sly humor surfaced in the 1837 publishing of *The Creole Village* in the literary magazine *The Magnolia.* He mocks our devotion to money and is credited as being first to use the phrase "the almighty dollar." "The almighty dollar, that great object of universal devotion throughout our land, seems to have no genuine devotees in these peculiar villages; and unless some of its missionaries penetrate there, and erect banking houses and other pious shrines, there is no knowing how long the inhabitants may remain in their present state of contented poverty."

Irving's trip through the prairies of the Mississippi River and the Arkansas River made him realize how much he wanted a place of his own. After having lived most of his adult life as a guest in other people's homes, the time had come for Irving to create his own space and settle down.

Irving wrote that he was eager for a home and was "willing to pay a little unreasonably for it."

Wolfert Acker, a Dutch American colonialist, lived in Tarrytown, New York. He owned a riverfront property on the banks of the Hudson River which was part of Philipsburg Manor and which, among other buildings, contained a simple two-room stone tenant farmhouse. The Van Tassel family, relatives of the Acker family, acquired the property and kept it until 1802, when another descendant of Wolfert, Maria Acker, was deeded 150 acres. Irving purchased the property on June 7, 1835, for $1,800. He later described it as "a beautiful spot capable of being a little paradise." He wanted to create a "little nookery in the Dutch style, quaint, but unpretending." Irving's neighbor and good friend, famous Scottish painter Sir George Frederick Harvey, provided valuable input and support during the restoration and expansion of the estate. Through the years, Irving expanded the property and enhanced the house by adding Tudor-style chimneys, Dutch stepped gables, Gothic windows, and a Spanish tower inspired by the famous Alhambra in Granada. The west facade of the house and the porch, which Irving called the "piazza," offered wonderful views of the Hudson River. The original house dates from the 1690s; no one knows the exact meaning of the "1656" Irving had inscribed at the top of one of the walls. The landscaping was done in a Romantic style. Irving transformed the grounds, planting trees, creating hills, and adding a charming pond he named "the little Mediterranean" and a waterfall leading to a meandering stream. The public interest in America's first literary celebrity drew numerous visitors throughout the years, hoping to catch a glimpse of Irving at work. Sunnyside, as

The Spanish tower added four bedrooms to the house.

it came to be known, served as a meeting place for the leading writers, politicians, artists, and other influential people of his era, including English author Charles Dickens and his wife. Irving's cottage was widely known at the time. It was publicized throughout the world in lithographs, tourist maps, magazines, and even *Harper's Weekly*. Irving, who never married or had children, shared Sunnyside for the next twenty-five years with his brother Ebenezer and his daughters. They supervised the running of the household. During those years, when Irving was away from home, traveling or assuming diplomatic obligations, he knew he had a well-cared-for home to return to, and a family waiting for him.

Images of Sunnyside were reproduced on cigar boxes, music sheets, and ceramics.

The house required constant and costly repairs and renovations. In order to meet these financial obligations, Irving reluctantly agreed to become a regular contributor to *The Knickerbocker* magazine, writing short stories and essays under the Crayon and Knickerbocker pseudonyms.

> *"There is a serene and settled majesty to woodland scenery that enters into the soul and delights and elevates it, and fills it with noble inclinations."*

In 1842, to the surprise of Irving and with the backing of Secretary of State Daniel Webster, President John Tyler nominated Irving as minister to the court of Isabella II of Spain, a position we would now call ambassador. Irving anticipated his new position would give him time to write, but his official duties as Spanish minister kept him very busy. He was involved in negotiating American trade interests with Cuba, following the Spanish parliament's debates over slave trade, and assisting in negotiating the Anglo-

Irving wrote: "It will be a severe trial to absent myself for a time from my dear little Sunnyside, but I shall return to it better enabled to carry it on comfortably."

American disagreement over the Oregon border that President James K. Polk wanted to resolve. During Irving's time in office, Spain was facing never-ending political turbulence and social turmoil, but Irving was always able to maintain close contacts with various influential Spanish politicians. Irving found the politics and warfare exhausting. Longing for his home, and suffering from an incapacitating skin disorder, he felt dispirited and demoralized.

In 1846, Irving left Spain and took up permanent residence at Sunnyside, where he began writing several biographies. In 1859, Irving wrote a biography of the eighteenth-century Irish novelist, playwright, and poet Oliver Goldsmith, best known for his novel *The Vicar of Wakefield*. Irving then focused on a third biography, *Life of Mohammed*, the story of the Islamic prophet and founder of the Islam faith. Irving wrote that according to Mohammed, the one true religion was revealed

Irving completed a five-volume biography of George Washington, researching in Mount Vernon and Washington, D.C., where he met with Presidents Fillmore and Pierce.

to five great prophets before him: Adam, Noah, Abraham, Moses, and Jesus. Yet people disregarded their teaching, choosing to revere false gods instead. Mohammed's objective was to abolish idolatry and to become the greatest prophet of the one and only God. His mission was initially unsuccessful in Mecca, but in the city of Medina his disciples grew in number, following his direction to walk to the desert and disseminate the word of God. Irving mixes legends and traditions and uses a flowing narrative to summarize Mohammed's faith, his spiritual teaching, and military conquests, including the invasion of Spain in 710 by his followers.

In 1855, Irving wrote *"Wolfert's Roose and Miscellanies,"* a collection of stories and essays first published in *The Knickerbocker* magazine.

"Great minds have purpose, others have wishes. Little minds are tamed and subdued by misfortunes, but great minds rise above them."

Irving maintained an active social life

well into his seventies. His celebrity and popularity continued to rise. In a letter to Irving, Senator William C. Preston wrote: "I don't believe that any man, in any country, has ever had a more affectionate admiration for him than that given to you in America." In 1859, Associate Justice of the Supreme Court Oliver Wendell Holmes Sr. wrote of Sunnyside: "It is next to Mount Vernon, the best known and most cherished of all the dwellings in our land." Irving was so popular and loved that a few years before his death, the village of Dearman, New York, voted to change its name to Irvington to honor him. Local residents pressed upon the Hudson River Railroad to change the name of their train station to Irvington.

Writers and critics throughout the nineteenth and twentieth centuries often referred to Irving as "the ambassador the New World sent to the Old."

In 1858, Irving was asked to participate in the celebration marking the placing of a telegraph cable across the Atlantic Ocean. It was a proper homage for a writer whose life and work had spanned both continents.

On November 28, 1859, on the eve of the Civil War, the father of American literature died of heart failure, surrounded by his family, at Sunnyside. He was seventy-six years old. His last words were said to be: "Well, I must arrange my pillows for another night. If this could only end!" Irving was buried on December 1, 1859, in the Sleepy Hollow Cemetery, a fitting resting place.

The Irving family continued to live at Sunnyside until 1945. The estate was then sold to philanthropist John D. Rockefeller Jr., whose charitable objective was to restore and maintain historically significant properties along the Hudson River, preserving their cultural heritage.

Sunnyside was renovated and opened to the public in 1947.

Washington Irving was an American short story writer, essayist, biographer, historian, and diplomat. He is universally acknowledged as the first American "man of letters" and the first to support himself by his writing.